Cc

Bees use dancing, vibration, sight, touch, and pheromones (chemical substances produced by bees) to pass on information. The waggle, round, and tremble dances communicate vital information about gathering nectar or pollen, essential food sources for the bee colony. The waggle dance conveys quality, quantity, and distance from the food. The longer the dance, the further the distance to the source. The livelier the dance, the better the nectar source. By angling her body in the appropriate direction, she tells her coworkers the exact direction to fly. Amazingly, she uses the sun as a directional locator. The round dance is typically used to convey a nearby food source. The tremble or vibrational dance alerts the work force when foragers are bringing in nectar fast. The returning scout bee, whose role is to find food sources, may dance in figure eights and circles while vibrating her body.

Honey bees have 15 glands that have been identified for specific uses. These glands produce "chemical messages," passing along information about things such as danger or safety; behavior prompts for wax making, swarming, homecoming, and helping in the manufacturing of protein-rich larval nutrition; and, most important, the health and location of the queen.

C is for Communication

With their bottoms in the air
as they dance on the comb,
it's the bees' way of saying,
"Hey, this is our home."

Brood are all the stages of the developing bee—the egg, larvae, and pupae. From egg to adult stages, the queen will mature in 16 days, a female worker in 21, and a drone in 24. Nurse bees feed the larvae about 1,000 times per day. They are given royal jelly (see letter R) for the first three days, and then for the rest of their development they are fed a nutritious mixture of honey and pollen (pollen is a substance produced by seed-bearing plants), which is called bee bread. The queen larva is also fed by the nurse bees, but her diet consists only of royal jelly.

The hive's temperature is controlled by the bees. It is kept between 93–96°F (about 35°C). If the hive gets too cold, the bees form a warming cluster around the brood, shivering their bodies to create warmth. If it's too hot, the bees fan their wings to cool the hive. Heater bees have a special purpose. They can increase their body temperature up to 111°F (44°C), nearly 10 degrees hotter than a normal bee. This extra heat is specifically used within the brood nest to maintain the perfect temperatures for the developing bee pupae.

B b

B is for Brood

Egg, larvae, and pupae
     are the stages of the brood.
The workers are responsible
     for feeding them sweet food.

Aa

A is for *Apis mellifera*

Apis is the clue that
we're talking about a bee.
And *mellifera* means
it's all about honey.

Apis florea

Apis mellifera

Apis dorsata

Apis

Honey bees are social insects working together for the health of the colony. A colony is the family unit with one queen, workers, and drones all living harmoniously in the hive.

There are about 11 species of honey bees. Four common species are *Apis mellifera* (European honey bee), *Apis florea* (dwarf honey bee), *Apis dorsata* (giant honey bee), and *Apis cerana* (Asian hive honey bee).

The average size of a healthy productive hive is about 60,000 bees with one egg-laying queen (but sometimes two). The majority of the population are female workers, who do a variety of ever-changing jobs. The smallest percentage of bees are the males (drones), whose only function is to mate with a queen.

Honey bees are not native to the United States. Ship records show that honey bees were brought to North America as early as the 1620s!

A Honey Bee's Body—Some Basics!

Honey bees have three main body parts: the head, the thorax, and the abdomen.

On the head there are two sensitive antennae, five eyes (two compound eyes and three smaller ocelli in the middle of the head), a proboscis (tongue) used for grooming and gathering nectar and water, and very strong mandibles (jaws).

The thorax has three pairs of legs and two pairs of wings.

The abdomen contains the reproductive organs, the wax glands, and a stinger. The body is covered with bristly hairs. Pollen sticks to these hairs as the bee flies from flower to flower.

Dd

D is for Drone

The drones are the males
of the bee colony.
Their life in the hive
is pretty easy.

Larger than the female worker, the drone is stocky. Because it is bigger, even the cell it grows in is larger. Drones do not have a stinger and their eyes are twice the size of workers' eyes to help them locate a virgin queen. A drone's sole purpose is to locate and mate with a virgin queen. Every day the drone leaves the hive and flies to a drone congregation area (also called a DCA) in search of a virgin queen. Drones from hundreds of colonies gather at these sites far from their own colony. The distance the queen must fly assures she does not mate within her own family. Matings occur midair, and after a drone mates with a queen, he will die. If he is unable to locate a queen, he will return to the hive and try again the next day. These DCA sites are smaller than an acre and are used every year.

Drones are incapable of feeding themselves or foraging for food. They live about three months. By fall, when the weather cools and food becomes scarce, the workers kick the males out to die of cold or starvation. The extra mouths to feed over the winter would be a drain on the hive.

E

E is for Egypt

Ancient is a word
that means "very, very old."
Proof of ancient beekeepers
are found in Egypt's relics and gold.

The earliest evidence of organized beekeeping is around 2400 BC, 4,500 years ago. Found on hieroglyphs in the sun temple of Pharaoh Ne-user-re near Cairo, Egypt, an Egyptian peasant is depicted smoking stacked hives while other workers are storing and sealing honey in jars. These ancient beehives were cylindrical and made of clay with interwoven twigs and reeds. It has been recorded that Egyptians also practiced migratory beekeeping. Special rafts were built to move hives up and down the Nile River to provide the bees with a continual source of nectar and pollen. This is similar to today's commercial beekeepers, who transport their bees across the country to pollinate crops like almonds, blueberries, and pumpkins.

Honey, or the ancient Egyptian *aba-t* or *bit*, was important to the Egyptians for several reasons. It was used for food, medicine, bartering, and even paying taxes.

Mummies were embalmed in wax and honey, and honey was left in tombs as food for the afterlife. Bees were a symbol of royalty. When King Tut's tomb was opened, 2,000-year-old jars of honey were found; they were still edible since honey never spoils. The two jars found were labeled as "honey of good quality" for his travel to the afterlife.

A bee can visit up to 5,000 flowers in a single day. The shape, smell, color, and movement are what attract the bee to the flower. When a bee flies, its body picks up a positive static charge. When it lands on a flower (which has a negative charge), the pollen is drawn to her body, clinging to her tiny hairs. Using her forelegs, she sweeps the pollen to pollen baskets on her hind legs. When her baskets are full, she will return to the hive to pack the protein-rich pollen into cells. Mixed with saliva and nectar or honey, it ferments and becomes bee bread, a primary food for developing larvae and adult bees. Bee bread contains microbes to help keep the colony healthy.

Pollination is the way a plant reproduces. When a bee collects pollen and nectar from a blossom, the pollen sticks to her body hairs. When she flies to the next flower, some of that pollen is rubbed off and will fertilize the new flower to make seeds. Pollen is the primary protein source collected for the young bees. A single hive of bees will travel 55,000 miles and visit two million flowers to make one pound of honey. Bees pollinate as many as 130 different crops in the United States alone, including fruits, vegetables, and tree nuts.

Ff

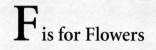

F is for Flowers

When the bee leaves her hive,
she's got one thing on her mind:
the "food" she'll collect from
the flowers she will find.

Gg

G is for Guard

They keep their hive safe
from robbers and thieves
like skunks, birds, or bears.
Only family members, please!

When the honey bee is about three weeks old, her job is to guard any entrances to the hive. As she stands on her hind feet, she smells each bee entering the hive. If it doesn't smell like family, she will do whatever it takes to keep the intruders out. If she needs extra help, she will release an alarm pheromone to call for help. If a human or animal threatens a hive, sometimes an entire hive comes to the rescue, all in order to defend the queen, the nursery, and the honey.

A weak hive can be completely robbed of its honey by wasps, other honey bees, or threats, such as mammals or humans. Without honey, the hive will die.

A foraging worker will not intentionally sting humans. She is too busy collecting nectar or pollen. Only in defense of the hive do honey bees become aggressive.

The honey bee is the only insect that makes food that humans can eat. Since honey bees usually make and store more honey than the colony needs, beekeepers are able to take just enough for themselves, leaving plenty for the survival of the hive. When it is fully cured and sealed, honey never spoils.

Raw honey is loaded with nutrients like energizing B vitamins, minerals, amino acids, and vitamin C. It contains antibacterial and antioxidant properties that help keep our immune system strong. Honey mixed with pollen (bee bread) contains all the essential components for a bee's life.

Honey isn't just good to eat. It is very effective for treating wounds and burns because most harmful bacteria cannot live in honey for any length of time. Honey has many uses: it's used in medicines to heal wounds and soothe sore throats; it's in foods like your morning cereal or yogurt; and, as a natural humectant (the ability to hold on to water), it is used as a moisturizer in cosmetics.

Hh

H is for Honey

Honey is sweet,
but it is so much more.
It's good medicine
from nature's drugstore.

I is for Insulation

When the weather turns cold,
the bees start to shiver.
The temperature is controlled
as their wings vibrate and quiver.

Ii

Honey bees do not hibernate over the winter. When the temperature falls below 57°F (13.89°C), the bees cluster into a ball in the hive just under where the honey is stored. The queen stops laying eggs and the workers focus on insulating the colony.

Bees closest to the center of the cluster feed on the stored honey. The outer layer of workers acts as an insulator. The colder the temperature, the tighter the cluster. Then the bees start to shiver. They vibrate their flight muscles, raising their body temperature. As thousands of bees continue shivering, the temperature at the center of the cluster warms up to about 93°F (34°C). When the workers on the outside of the cluster get cold, they switch places with those on the inside. This warming continues all winter long, keeping the queen and brood warm.

It is critical that the colony maintains the perfect temperature. Just as the bees can control the cold, they can also work to reduce the heat. If the hive is too hot, the bees will fan their wings to ventilate it.

J is for Job

From tending the nursery
to minding the queen,
each bee is important,
each job is supreme.

The honey bee hive is a harmonious society, working together for the colony's survival. In the hive all the workers are infertile females. The fertile queen will spend her entire life laying eggs in the hive, and the drones' only function is to mate with a queen.

Worker bees share jobs based on their age. For instance, worker bees that are one to two days old spend their time cleaning cells. Bees between the ages of three to sixteen days may work as undertakers, removing dead bees from the hive, while others will work in the nursery, tending to the brood and the queen. As these nurse bees mature, their queen-tending jobs will vary from feeding, cleaning, and grooming her to spreading her queen pheromone throughout the hive and even removing her waste from the hive. Before they leave the hive as foragers, workers are responsible for producing wax, building comb, maintaining the hive's temperature, and drying the nectar. At 18–21 days old, they get guard duty, protecting the hive entrance. From 22 days on, until their death at around 40–45 days, they are field and scout bees, collecting pollen, nectar, and water and making propolis.

All these jobs can be done at varying ages, depending on the needs of the hive.

J j

K k

K is for Keeper

A beekeeper can be anyone—
man, woman, or kid.
Practice patience and purpose
when you pop open the "lid."

Anyone can become a beekeeper, or apiculturist. The best way to learn is from an experienced beekeeper. Beekeepers have a special bond with their bees. By caring for honey bees, they help put fruit, vegetables, and nuts on our table.

The commercial beekeeper's livelihood depends on their bees. Though honey production is important, pollination is a big part of the income. Truckloads of active beehives are driven considerable distances to pollinate crops that do not have enough local bees to do the work. Their large business requires forklifts, tractor trailers, huge honey-extraction work sites, and extra workers. The hobbyist beekeeper may have between two and two hundred hives and focuses on honey and wax production as well as pollinating nearby crops.

Honey bee pollination has an agricultural value of 20 billion dollars a year in the United States and is the primary income for commercial beekeepers. They pollinate about 30 percent of the crops that we eat.

It is important for the survival of the honey bee to have more responsible hobby beekeepers. Pests, diseases, pesticides, and loss of natural food sources are killing our bees. We can all help by planting more bee-friendly plants, trees, and flowers.

L is for Langstroth

Lorenzo Langstroth
invented a hive
with the health of the honey bee
in mind.

Born on Christmas Day in 1810, Lorenzo Lorraine Langstroth is known as the father of humane, practical beekeeping. He was a minister who took up beekeeping to help with his bouts of depression. In 1851 he discovered "bee space," a roughly one-centimeter-wide passage that allowed bees to move and work freely around the edges of the comb. After discovering this space, he designed a hive that allowed beekeepers to manage the bees' health and harvest the honey. The bees could build their honey-combs on each frame without sticking to one another, making it easier to remove or replace each frame. All this could be done without upsetting the bees or damaging the combs. Before movable frames, bees built permanent combs inside their hives, making it necessary to destroy the bees and their hive to harvest the honey.

Langstroth's invention led to further inventions by others. For example, the modern smoker, used to calm bees while working the individual frame, was invented by Moses Quinby in 1873. These and many other tools (see letter T) were invented all because of one man's hobby with bees.

Ll

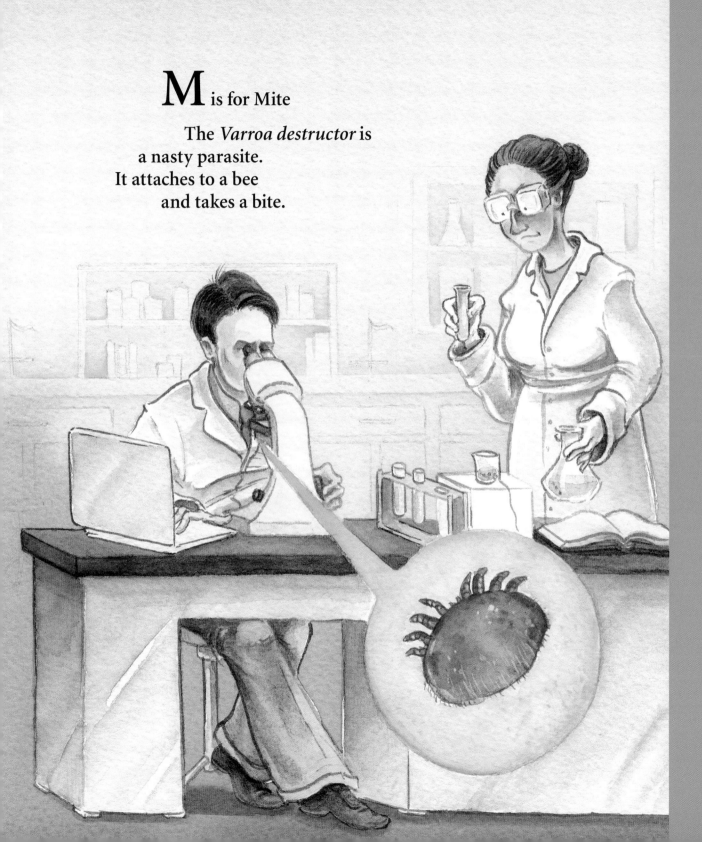

M is for Mite

The *Varroa destructor* is
a nasty parasite.
It attaches to a bee
and takes a bite.

The *Varroa* mite, also known as the vampire mite, is a ticklike insect that has a flat, crablike body with eight legs. It is about the size of a pinhead. Despite its tiny size, it can be responsible for killing an entire hive. It was discovered in the United States in 1987 and is found almost worldwide.

These mites will attach themselves to a bee and feed on the fat body tissue. After feeding, a female mite will enter an uncapped cell that contains a developing larva. The pool of rich royal jelly keeps her hidden until the cell is sealed. When the cell is capped, she comes out of hiding, attaches to the larva, and feeds, compromising the larva's immune system and development. Now well fed, the female mite will lay several eggs. When the young mites hatch in the sealed cell, they continue to feed on the larva, developing alongside it. When the bee is fully developed, it chews its way out of the cell. The mites escape, too. Roaming the hive, the young mites attach themselves and feed off adult bees, and the process starts anew.

Affected bees have shortened lives and will unintentionally pass on mites and possibly diseases to the rest of their hive and nearby hives.

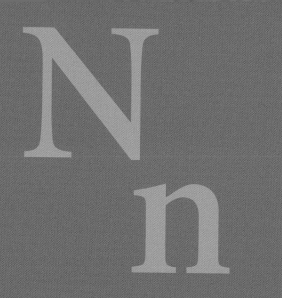

N n

N is for Nectar

Nectar is collected
and brought back to the hive.
Once processed into honey,
it's what helps the bees thrive.

Nectar is sugary water found in the base of flowers, which honey bees drink. It is an important energy source for the bees and brood.

Field bees, or foraging bees, collect nectar by sucking it up with their proboscis (a strawlike tongue) and storing it in their honey stomach, or crop (a unique stomach with special enzymes). When the crop is full, the bee returns to the hive, transferring the nectar to a hive bee, where it mixes with the enzymes in her honey crop. The forager bee leaves to collect more nectar while the hive bees begin a "sharing" process to cure the nectar. The hive bees regurgitate the nectar among themselves over and over again until the enzymes from their saliva break down the sugar content and reduce the moisture content from about 90 percent to about 20 percent. This sharing can take up to 20 minutes. The nectar is then deposited into cells. Fanning bees will further reduce the honey to about 18 percent. The cured honey is then sealed with a thin layer of wax to keep it from spoiling.

Nectar from different flowers produces different flavored honey. Linden tree blossoms are well known for producing a minty honey.

An observation hive is a beehive placed between glass panels. This makes it perfect for bee watching without fear of being stung. These hives can be attached to a wall, mounted on a table, or they can be portable.

Portable observation hives contain only a few frames of bees. They are temporary and lightweight and can be taken to classrooms for educational visits. Indoor observation hives are permanently installed and are home to an entire working hive. An attached travel tube to the outside allows these bees safe passage to and from the hive. These hives are often found in educational and nature centers.

Observation hives let us see the bees' busy lives. You can watch the queen lay eggs, workers fan moisture from the nectar, and observe the bees dancing on the comb. You can also see the special bees that attend the queen, and watch how field bees return to the hive and pass off the nectar to receiver bees.

Observation hives reveal the hidden lives of bees and some behaviors can only be observed this way. An example is festooning, which is when a chain of bees link together for the purpose of cell construction.

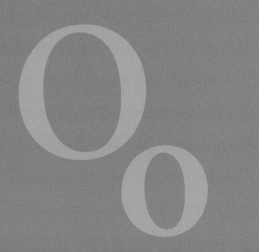

O is for Observation Hive

Take a peek
            inside this hive.
Watch now as
        it comes alive.

P is for Propolis

Every nook, cranny, and crevice
is glued tight with propolis.
Trees provide this sticky sap
that bees can use as a mousetrap.

Propolis is a mixture of plant resins, wax, oils, pollen, and bee saliva. As far back as 300 BC, the Greeks and Egyptians used propolis, or bee glue, as antiseptics to kill germs. Special forager bees collect sap produced by plants and trees to waterproof and strengthen their hives. Bees use their forelegs and mandibles to collect it. As workers collect the sap, they mix it with wax secreted from wax glands. They then knead this into a small ball and store it in the pollen basket. Returning to the hive, they pass it on to a house bee, who works it with more wax and saliva. They chew the propolis until it is soft and pliable and ready to be placed where it is needed.

Its special antibacterial and antifungal qualities help stop bacteria and fungus. It helps protect the hive from unwanted visitors such as mice, mold, moths, and beetles. Bees corner and imprison insects with the sticky sap. If a mouse somehow finds its way into the hive and dies, the bees encase the body in propolis to mummify it, thus preventing its decay from contaminating the hive. Like honey, propolis has been used as a medicinal treatment for wounds and burns. It is also used as an ingredient in chewing gum, toothpaste, cosmetics, and ointments.

Q is for Queen

All hail queen bee!
For she can lay
about two thousand
eggs in just a day.

A fertile queen is the largest bee in the hive. If a hive is not queenright, with a healthy egg-laying queen, the entire hive may fail. Reduced or absent queen pheromone will alert the colony of a failing or dead queen. Immediately, workers select fertile eggs to begin the process of raising a replacement queen. Several potential queens grow in cells that look like peanut shells (called supersedure cells) that are often located near the middle of the comb.

During the larval stage, potential queens are fed only royal jelly. Sixteen days later a virgin queen emerges from her cell. The first thing she does is locate and kill any unhatched rival queens. She will begin piping and tooting to communicate to the hive that she is born.

Usually within a week she will leave the hive for her mating flights. She flies to a distant drone congregation area, and over the next several days she may mate with 12 to 20 drones. After successfully mating she has two main purposes: lay eggs and produce pheromones. Her pheromones ensure the unity of the hive by affecting the colony's social behavior and maintenance of the hive. She can lay up to 2,000 eggs a day.

Qq

Rr

R is for Royal Jelly

Royal jelly is
a super food.
A little is fed
to the brood.

Young worker bees secrete a protein-rich royal jelly (bee milk) from the hypopharyngeal gland in their head. It is a milky substance that contains about 60 percent water, 18 percent proteins, 12 percent sugar, and small amounts of fats, vitamins, salts, and amino acids.

All honey bee larvae are fed royal jelly. It is like a super-nutritious kick start to their development. After several days the worker and drone bee larvae are switched to nectar and bee bread, a mixture of honey and pollen. Only the queen larvae will continue to be fed royal jelly. It is this diet that extends the queen's life to two to five years. A worker's life span is only six weeks. It is called royal jelly because it is the primary diet for the queen.

Royal jelly can be found in skin care products and herbal supplements.

Swarming is how a honey bee hive creates a new colony. In early spring, when nectar and pollen are abundant, the queen begins to lay eggs again. The hive can double or triple in size from 10,000 bees to 30,000–40,000 bees by late spring, early summer. If the hive is so crowded with brood that the queen has no place to lay eggs, she will lay fertile eggs in existing starter queen cells (queen cups). These swarm cells are located near the bottom of the frames.

The queen continues to lay eggs while workers tend to the developing queen cells. Workers reduce the queen's food and exercise her more to strengthen her and slim her down for the swarming flight. When the time is right, and the new queen cells are sealed, the queen will leave the hive, taking about half of the colony with her. The swarm settles on a nearby branch while scout bees look for a new home.

The scouts return to the resting cluster with information on several possible sites. When the scouts agree on the most desirable location, a signal is given and they guide the swarm to their new home. In effect, the colony has just reproduced itself, and the original queen has left the old hive forever.

S s

S is for Swarm

When a hive becomes overpopulated,
a daughter queen may be created.
The old queen leaves with half of the hive.
One hive becomes two and both will survive.

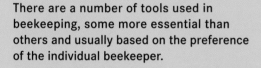

T is for Tools

To work with your bees
you'll need special tools.
The brush, veil, and smoker—
to name just a few.

There are a number of tools used in beekeeping, some more essential than others and usually based on the preference of the individual beekeeper.

Many beekeepers say that the smoker is the most important tool. Bellows pump air through a pot containing smoking debris. A few puffs of cool smoke calm the defensive nature of bees and mask the alarm pheromone. Hive inspection is much easier with smoke. A hive tool is a seven- to twelve-inch flattened piece of steel and is essential to pry apart frames and supers (individual boxes above the brood chambers storing excess honey) that have been glued tight with propolis. A soft bristled bee brush is used to gently brush the bees off the frames during inspection. Protective clothing is a personal choice. Some beekeepers do not wear any protective gear; others cover from head to toe with gloves, a veil, pants, and a jacket. The extractor is an electric or hand-cranked barrel-shaped tank with special baskets inside that hold two or more honey frames, which are spun at high speed. The spinning flings the honey from the frames to the inside walls of the barrel, where it drains down to the bottom to be tapped out and bottled.

Finally, it is essential to keep records, or bee journals, each time a hive is inspected.

Urban beekeeping is the practice of keeping bees in a city environment, and it requires special bee etiquette. Although statistics vary, urban beekeepers number up to 120,000 in America. It is important to follow city and state laws when setting up an apiary. Building a solid fence or growing hedges around the hive will train the bees' flight pattern up and over the fence line to help avoid human and animal contact. Rooftop apiaries, backyard garden plots, and neighborhood community gardens are common in big cities and are all spaces that can be occupied by beehives.

Bees are big water drinkers, so to prevent them from invading the neighbor's pool, you should always have fresh water available. A water fountain is not only enjoyable for humans but the bees love it, too. The honey bee usually forages three to five miles for nectar and pollen. Cities have an abundance of flowering trees and plants offering a continuous source of food. In the United States a vast amount of the honey production comes from weeds in abandoned city lots and fields. When these fields and city lots are plowed under or paved over, an important source of bee food disappears.

U is for Urban Beekeeping

If there's plenty of
food, water, and sun,
city bees can be
lots of fun!

U u

A worker bee's barbed stinger is at the end of her abdomen and is attached to the poison sac. The worker bee usually starts producing venom (also called apitoxin) at about 14 days old. When the bee stings an animal or human, it leaves behind its stinger, ripping out its digestive tract, muscles, and nerves, thus killing the bee. Unless removed, the intact stinger continues to pump apitoxin into the victim for up to 10 minutes. Because of released attack pheromones, one stinging bee could lead to more attacking bees that will often sting at or near the original sting location.

Drones do not have a stinger. The queen's stinger does not have a barb, so she can sting multiple times but rarely does. Because she has no enemies in her hive and her safety is a top priority for the colony, the queen has little need for a stinger. Honey bees that are away from the hive rarely sting and are focused only on foraging pollen, nectar, propolis, or water. Only threatened bees will sting. They are attracted by quick movements, so try to stay calm and quiet if you encounter one. Most often when people report being stung by bees, they are actually stung by wasps, yellow jackets, or hornets.

V
v

V is for Venom

Venom is the toxin
that comes from her stinger.
It may cause painful swelling
and an itch that might linger.

W

W is for Wax

On the underside of a bee
(though it is rather hard to see)
is a gland for making wax
for building comb and sealing cracks.

When honey bees are between 12 and 20 days old, they develop four pairs of wax glands on the underside of their abdomen. These glands produce wax scales, which are transferred to the front legs. Bees use their antennae, mandibles, and legs to soften and form the wax. Once the wax is ready, the bees form it into hexagon-shaped cells in which to store honey. The hexagon shape requires the least amount of wax for the most amount of honey storage space.

Wax cells conduct bee vibration, so the comb is thought of as the biggest organism in the hive because of its ability to help communicate the needs of the colony.

During the hard work of honey extraction, a special knife is used to trim away the thin layer of wax used to seal the honey in the cells. This wax is then cleaned and melted down to be used for a variety of products.

Beeswax is used to make candles, salves, furniture polish, lip balms, cosmetics, and soaps, as well as other products.

Like airplanes landing at an airport, bees have their own runways. The traffic is orderly and efficient. Field bees fly in and out of the hive from sunup until sundown, carrying in nectar and pollen. Standard hives have one long narrow entrance at the bottom and a smaller entrance under the top cover; this offers ventilation from top to bottom. The bottom entrance can be reduced during the winter to keep the hive warmer and to prevent mice and shrews from making the hive their winter home.

At the peak of a nectar flow, when blossoms are abundant and full of nectar, bees fly back and forth in a frenzied and continuous flow without congestion or mishap. During a dearth, when forage is scarce, the bee traffic is slow.

A longtime mystery that remains unsolved is a behavior called washboarding. Rows of bees rock back and forth at the hive entrance. While the exact reason for washboarding isn't known, there are many theories, from cleaning and smoothing the surface of the entrance to cooling and communicating to the hive.

Xx

X is for Exit (and Entrance)

Don't stand in front of the hive
as the bees fly in and out.
They have a precise flight pattern
as they fly their direct route.

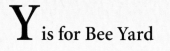

Y is for Bee Yard

Stacked close together
or very far apart,
the apiary is a bee neighborhood
that anyone can start.

Yy

A bee yard (also called an apiary) is a place where beehives are kept. A yard's location is very important to successful beekeeping. There are many factors beekeepers need to consider. These include: food and water sources for the hives; easy access to the yards for the beekeepers to work and observe the hives; shade for hot climates, wind breaks for cold and snowy conditions; and an east-facing hive entrance so the bees get the first morning light for an early start to their work day.

In addition to the Langstroth hive, other styles are the top bar hive and the Warre (pronounced WAR-ray) hive. Both of these were designed to mirror the natural cavity of a hive. The top bar is long like a log and the Warre is tall like a tree. They are foundationless, so the bees build their own comb.

Commercial beekeepers transport the bees and their hives to nectar and pollen sources. These traveling hives pollinate large crops of fruit, nuts, and vegetables. Hobbyist beekeepers, with fewer hives, maintain permanent locations and must consider what their area will support. Too many bees in one area may mean not enough food for the bees.

Bees vibrate their bodies and wing muscles to make the buzzing sound that we hear. Honey bees have wings about the size of their abdomen and beat them about 230 times a second or 13,800 beats per minute.

Bees buzz for many reasons. Pressing your ear flat against the outside of the hive will reveal much just by listening. A relaxed hum means the hive is content. A louder buzz may mean they are angry or annoyed. When a colony has been without a queen for a while, their temperament is angry and their buzz is loud. An egg-laying queen is crucial to the colony's survival. Without her, the hive remains unsettled until a new queen is made. You may even be able to hear the piping, tooting, and quacking sounds of a virgin queen.

A steady buzz can be heard as bees use their fanning wings to cool the hive or remove moisture from the stored nectar. During colder months, as the colony clusters to stay warm, you'll hear the soothing hum of thousands of vibrating wings.

Zz

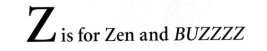

Z is for Zen and *BUZZZZ*

There's a whole lotta sound
coming from the hive.
Listen closely to know
what is going on inside.